FORGETTING TO COME IN

Paul McLoughlin

Shoestring Press

Typeset and Printed by Parker and Collinson Ltd.
Nottingham NG7 2FH
(0115) 942 0140

Published by Shoestring Press
19 Devonshire Avenue, Beeston, Nottingham, NG9 1BS
(0115) 925 1827
www.shoestringpress.co.uk

First Published 2007
© Paul McLoughlin
The moral right of the author has been asserted.

ISBN: 978 1 904 886 52 5

Shoestring Press gratefully acknowledges financial assistance from
Arts Council England.

ACKNOWLEDGEMENTS

Many of these poems first appeared (sometimes in earlier versions) in the following publications to whose editors grateful acknowledgement is made: *Anon; Atlas; Critical Survey; Cyphers (Ireland); The Frogmore Papers; Hard Times (Germany); The Interpreter's House; Magma; Nightingale; Other Poetry; Penniless Press; Poetry Life; The Rialto; Southword (Ireland); Tears in the Fence; Wandering Dog.*

'African Negatives', 'Flugel' and 'Listen Here' appeared in *Paging Doctor Jazz* (Shoestring Press, 2004). 'The End of British Farming' and 'The Man They Named After His Bed' appeared in the Worple Press anthology, *Warp and Weft* (2007). 'The End of Goodbyes' won second prize in *The New Writer* collection competition 2004.

I am particularly indebted to John Forth and Trish Bull, my principal first readers, for their painstaking attention and better judgement.

I also thank Helen Tobin for providing the definitive translation of the Gaelic rhyme that forms the epigraph to 'The End of Goodbyes'.

'Six for Cricket' was commissioned for the Bedford Park Festival 2004.

For Nina & Thomas

Contents

THE END OF GOODBYES

Murreigh, Easter 1996

Baile na nGall,
Baile cois Abhain,
Baile beag briste,
Lamh le h-uisce,
Agus mna gan tuiscint ann.

Ballydavid,
House by the river,
Small broken house,
With the water at hand,
And the women who don't understand.

James and Mary

He'd known too many people who
were looking well and they're all dead.
At his age you believe your feet
are carrying you along, but they're going
nowhere. He was still translating
from the Gaelic when he spoke,
in tears with Mary, looking for a sign
his sister would remember she'd
been here at all.
                    He made me chase
the census man for an English version –
England was a marvellous place with its
money and its education.
                    "Qualifications?"
Mary said. "Put that we went to school
and came home again all those years ago."

The Road to Baile na nGall

Was it because we picked up the car
at the airport's edge she thought
it was stolen? It was a long way
to drive, she worried, with the flight
forgotten. Everyone she meets
these days was born in Murreigh –
and she's waiting for James to arrive
from the football sixty years ago,
at eighty-eight and moving
gingerly.
        It wasn't for him
to tell her to get down off the wall
on the road to Baile na nGall with it
not yet dark. He wasn't her father
and it was something she'd not forget.

Maurice

Mother and Maurice were inseparable
until she went to Dublin at seventeen
and he to Chicago. Did he come back
to live alone in this see-through house
beside a nephew who's seen better days,
and the protestant church that lost
its bell, an old witch moving in
who could well be dead?
        We're looking
at a mounted plaque commemorating
thirty years in the City Housing Dept.
and a photograph with colleagues
showing him plumper. He came back
chewing, that's for sure, but he
couldn't be Maurice Malone.

The Monastery

No one remembers the monks, but once
this was a convent teeming with nuns.
Now it's a page of windows stuck
on a hill, an advent calendar of its own
demise, the youngest of its six sisters
seventy three. What can Ashe or Collins
do but go on opening their shops?
The auctioneer will come and they'll wait
and see, but God knows who will want
the place with its corridors and rooms.
James thinks it's to do with the telephone
and the outside getting in, like the end
of Latin. And what good could they ever do,
up there on the hill, with their holy lives?

Minard Castle

Stumble on these rocks, imagine
history happening, or at least your mother
in her youth. There were Vikings in the bay,
and Spanish refugees I'm told
we're related to – but Minard's more
modern than you'd think, its fissures
lightning cracks.
                        Marian thinks of Brighton
beach blown up a hundred times. She finds
the Sun of all things rolled up and wedged
against the wind, but Mum stays in the car
with forgotten faces. The holy terrors! Look at them
tripping over these shoe-shine boulders to the sea.
She made the one attempt and all but drowned.
Rain is battering the castle's warning plate.

Gallarus Oratory

Eye of the needle, my mother called it
as a girl, the arrow slit they crawled through
out into the fields and away, from the cro,
pre-Christian dry-stone beehive hut.
Over the stile and along the shifting
gravel path (not easy in your seventies!)
to a fancy plaque explaining this is
a refined version of what there are still
400 of.
        No chance now of squeezing
through. We laugh about the unfairness
of it all, for we are none of us rich –
but Mum's pre-occupied with a Gaelic
rhyme she's chanting over and over:
Baile na nGall, baile cos abhain . . .

Bridge and Johnny

No need to be locking the car with the door
of the house wide open. Inside, Bridge is
reeling in the years with Mum who smiles
and leans across to ask, "Are you Bridge
Connor?"
        Johnny Griffin's at the door
bellowing through bronchitis, naming
every clutch of houses in the valley and telling
of six in a boat and three canoes for salmon –
two thousand six hundred in two months once,
and a hundred and eleven in one haul!
Now you struggle to catch your breath,
but you couldn't forget.
        Tea and barmbrack
and the end of goodbyes, and the ride
back repeating, "Yes, Mum, that's Bridge."

LEGOLAND

You wake at midnight in a dream of trains
and lean against our bed, afraid. A track
stretches out across your strewn floor and back
beneath a chest of drawers, past tower cranes
in loading bays and queues of patient cars
that wait in vain for barriers to rise,
and passengers who never close their eyes
in sleep or dream or cuddle their bears.

You say explosions woke you, horrible
explosions you will dream again, you *know*.
Your high-speed inter-city's on its side,
derailed, with the current switched off. How local
fears accelerate in sleep and grow –
it was your coughing woke you; your dream lied.

FLAMES

Playing wall-tennis with the washing out was trouble
I could see, Mum reeling up the pulleyed line
of bruised whites squeaking their way to a clip
round the ear when Dad got home. As a rule
I wasn't quick at spotting danger – watching firemen
save each other over the wall on their practice tower
never somehow got me seeing flames –
but when I looked on Jacqueline Pavitt in the prefab
garden stretched out in a bikini, I knew what Mum
would think. She will have promised Mrs P
the unmentionable Catholic pamphlet I delivered,
once I'd sneaked a look. The important thing
about going steady, it said, was GO STEADY,
though I wouldn't have known what that meant.

A PURGE ON UNIFORM

In an interview once he'd enchanted one of the panel
by saying he didn't remember his own education
      in courses or whole-school policies,
he remembered lessons, even bits of lessons,
      and he wanted to teach one of those.

It wasn't enough. Now he's dressing down a lad
in the corridor for wearing high fashion to school –
      but he's forgiven him already
for his way with words, remembering a first-year
      poem in which the boy

had wondered whether the daytrippers dumping food
and crumpled cans were descended from those who'd brought
      sand to the beach and left it there.
He remembers too the gobsmacked silence
      when he'd read them Oedipus –

presumably, Jocasta wouldn't be seen in rags!
He sends him packing, stooping to pick up a chocolate
      wrapper then dropping it into
a nearby bin. He'd like to do the same
      to the National Curriculum,

which didn't realise standards had been falling since the Greeks –
or that what kept him going was the unaccountable belief
      that every now and again,
when he wasn't looking, someone would think
      about sand on a beach.

THE POEM

The performance, too, had been stunning,
one had to admit, whispered, hissed,
rising rarely from its *sotto voce* bed.

And the response adulatory – although
a bearded ex-Catholic, who would not be
bullied into awe, wondered what on earth

he was supposed to do with all this
mystical shit, this Vision of Redemption
that hadn't been written at all, but came.

Which is what she was threatening to do
on the festival floor. He returned her gaze
until his mouth pronounced a sudden

slow smile, his right knee turned out
like an open gate, his monstrous boots
laced at the insteps, flanged at the shins

like fleurs-de-lys and flapping at plumbed-in
jeans as he loped on his moonwalk
through King's Cross. I shouldn't say

the smile was knowing, or risk stoking
the fire raging in her cheeks – but this being
a poem, as they always are, about me,

or a part I play, I could have him,
in the stunned silence, nuzzle up to her,
and have her moan, because I've no way

of knowing whether he was as meretricious
as I was amused, and it would let me in
behind the mask to find an ordinary lie.

AT THE WATERMAN'S

1. *Little Voice*

Come Fly With Me. We should have known
this would be about homing pigeons
and human birds in search of flight,
a little voice that's silent when it's not
impersonating Garland, Monroe, Bassey

for the Dad who's dead, and Telephone Bill,
the heartthrob at her window, not on a ladder
but hoisted on a cherry-picker cantilevered
to his BT van. His precious Dwayne flies home
from Europe as we knew it would, but lands

on her window ledge, not his. We're watching
cinema's equivalent to all those first flutterings
in verse, children writing peoms about brids,
the spelling mistakes a kind of stumbling
into speech. She helps him exercise the birds.

2. *'Round Midnight*

Dexter Gordon's playing someone much like Dexter Gordon
thawing out in Paris, his *machinery* obsessed with saving
Gordon's sound and, with it, him. Europe loves its New York
legends, though they still play small on West Third Street.

A rock star said when Coltrane died it was a shame
he never made it. There's a clean-cut trio steaming in the bar
when we come out, and a jazz-freak in the foyer selling Monk.

3. *Il Postino*

You can book if you like, but Tuesday afternoon
for an Italian film with English subtitles
and a Chilean poet? There'll be no one there.

The place was packed. Latecomers were forced
apart by an old-age pilgrimage alive
to weekday rates – and no one made a sound.

This was new, an older generation better
educated than the young, better able
to look out for itself and, for all we knew, surprised

the local bookseller was not on hand
with a job lot of Neruda
specially bought in.

TWO POEMS ABOUT CROWDS

1.

After Hogarth

The pastor points to heaven, finger and fist, the 'prentice
reads his book of common prayer. Is he to be hanged
because he didn't give a hundred and ten per cent? It's
a struggle getting him there, despite the mounted guard,
chatting, upright, easing through the crowd, with carted coffin,
pastor and condemned, their pikes more than ceremonial
regalia. Is that a child spread out like a hearthed dog,
smoking a pipe on the waiting scaffold's beam? And who's this
standing with her back to the action, cradling a child
with the same hand that holds, unfurled, *The last dying Speech
& Confolation of Tho. Idle –*, like a programme-seller?
They're packed in temporary stands, a flat-capped infant
throwing a paper dove – or trying to catch a real one.
Others perch astride a high bricked wall, or clamber up
to a vantage point atop the carriage of a gentleman,
only to be whipped for the impertinence. A pet dog's
dangled like a pheasant by its tail, a fruit-vendor blinded
so his barrow rocks and spills its load. Girls throw bouquets.
When the body is cut down there'll be a rush to touch it.

2.

Today is match-day and the nearest station
miles away. Get there, faster, faster, look,
the road's dead straight from Seven Sisters –
ignore the pubs that spill into the street,

the touts with bulging vests who'll have no truck
with ditherers, the police on horseback
smiling till the need says otherwise. The noise
is pounding in your ears. You love this game.

What was the point of instruction even then?
These people never learn. The cost of winning
is spectacular and cruel, is met with
corporate hospitality and sponsorship,

the restaurant, the shop, some stuff for kids
and the community. It's the people's game
because they come to watch. You think it's heartless.
It's the only way. Let them read their rags

and others sell them tat. We're done with
explaining. The market mops up arguments
as bread mops *jus*. The players get too much,
of course, but there we are. It's how it is.

And some undo themselves. They're thrown
a damn sight more than improvised bouquets.
Let them imagine they are what they've been made.
They cry on relegation day like fans.

FROM THE SPANISH

I

My children let me talk. It takes me one-two-three sometimes more pushes to get up from the chair with my swollen leg. Sofas are the worst. I tell them everything. Today I bought some *chirimoyas* the barrow boy reminded me were custard-apples. I loved their sweet taste and didn't mind the pips. A neighbour changed the settings on my heater, saying no wonder my bills were high. Higher than my blood pressure, I said. Every time the doctor changes so do my pills. I've written to my sister in Madrid. She's fantastic and Victoriano's better since the double hernia. This letter I have from her was posted on the twenty-seventh, yesterday, and it arrived today. I've never been one for buying presents. I give my children money, let them choose for themselves. When I dream of them, the girls are both grown up, but my son I always dream of as a boy.

II

Seventeen days it took the boat to Greenock from Gibraltar in October 1943 because of mines. It was the war. We didn't know about the blackout or anything like that. We didn't see Glasgow, just went to the hotel and got the morning train. St Pancras wasn't pretty at all. He said *Tu verras mieux!* and left me in that big place like a croûte to find a telephone. I always sat with the *valises*. He took the children off to watch cartoons. Before our train they saw them three times through. Once, when little Nina needed changing, he wouldn't wait, went to Victoria and Brighton on his own. He was an *ours en cage*. So there you are.

13

III

How many times have I known nothing about the house or paying bills or
bringing up the children properly, though bringing up the children was my
job? My accent flusters me. I think of Spain, La Linea, Gibraltar, sixty
years ago. I still say foreinger and end my verbs in *ing*. The girls spoke
only French until they went to school. Then Jacques, my son, came back
from São Paulo with Portuguese. I went for English lessons but the
teacher held up a sandal he wanted me to call a shoe. Now my daughter
does the *paperasse* she calls it once a week. I keep the post until she
comes. She has put this right for me for her to read.

IV

Soup Cambel chiquen
1 tin consome mais cest
Black Welles Crosse
una tine de tuna
un paquet small tea Taately
un jard Nescafe Original small
4 paquet de jelly Rasbery
Green Lemon or Orange
et Black curret and
yogourt plain o Rasbery
une bataille de Jerez
paquet Noes Quze
chique Stock

PRIVATE SCREENINGS

The trouble with rhetoric
    is you have to be
on its side – the tragedy
not that they fell bravely
    but that they fell.

Hard-edged, practical men
    have no time
for adverbs. They know
the lessons of the dead
    lie unlearned,

the sparkling of their light
    tranquil and remote
as that of a star. No one
lives long enough to stop
    it happening again.

Texts inside survivors'
    heads conflict
with other texts – it isn't
fact we store but trauma,
    however it was.

That eighteenth of July
    we were in mourning
for my grandfather, the baker,
sad we couldn't celebrate
    La Feria.

Fireworks were Franco's
    guns from Africa.
Blood ran through the streets.
They took the garrison.
    We stayed indoors

and lived on Grandad's
    flour, flat tortillas
for weeks on end. Butchers'
knives were commandeered
    and they were right,

but Dad slipped out in Mother's
    clothes, like others
in the brotherhood, until
the women brought up children
    on their own,

and lived in fear, cheered only
    when the priest
was shot. That fascist anthem
introduced each film. We raised
    arms side by side.

In 'thirty-eight, Azaña said:
    When the torch passes
to other generations, other men,
if ever they feel their blood boil,
    and the Spanish temper

is once more infuriated
    with intolerance
and hatred and destruction,
let them think of the dead
    and listen to

the message of the eternal
    fatherland,
which says to all its sons:
Peace, Pity and Pardon.
    It makes me cry.

PHONETIC FAILURE

On the journey back from the Millennium
where Brentford played like drowsy bees
and lost, wipers flailing against the rain
and spray for a hundred miles, and over-
hauling long vehicles in what feels like
hope, we wonder what possessed us.
£48 for a football match,
for a pair of tickets to park and ride
to a sodden city centre cloned from other
city centres with McDonald's, M & S,
and a macho barmaid balancing a tower
of empties. Except I hadn't written
'pounds' on the cheque I posted to
your best friend's mum. "I hope
you think it's worth that many
'poems'," she said. My wife's
retrieved the thing and framed it,
hung it on the bedroom wall,
told everyone.

THE BALCONY

He flicks the pages of a book pulled from the box
as if it's showing him a movie of the plot.
He sighs, says what's the point of telling me.
The others have grown used to being cordoned off.
They miss their mates, from time to time look down or through
the window at whatever's there: a fag-ash wash,
white blossom surging over storm-porch roof,
a shortened view of trees, a branch that pirouettes
to silence, stands its brushes up against a wall
of sky. My turn to supervise them, keep them out
of circulation. They must be bored. He's simmering,
the wind is dead, the chart a swirl of isobars.

FRAGMENTS OF HUMANITY

On a woodcut by Hans Holbein

A cadaverous timpanist is stirring
thickly in a brace of deep tureens
soup that would sustain him were it soup.

He's hammering skins with gusto
in an orchestra of bones. Brass is hauled
somehow to the horizontal, breathed into life.

Skulls crowd the square to celebrate
the possibility of air. One weighed down
with keyboard and the mallet that's clipped on

is wearing shades under a ringlet wig; another's
resting humerus on knee to smoke a horn.
There are occasional hats and limp intestines.

They're playing for all they're worth.
When they disperse, disintegrate,
charitable fumigators will move in.

CHILDREN OF THE SUN

Granting these people places on
our course is reckless of
the fuss they make of words.
Agreed, it isn't wise to turn down
anyone with a degree
of aptitude and I admit they can
write, but poets have no
stomach for the elasticity of
truth we're looking for. Bonking
celebs a pair of compasses?
This kind of stuff won't wash,
and no self-respecting writer'd
get out of bed for what a poet
calls an audience. We're talking
breakfast tables here and over-
crowded tubes and comfort breaks,
so I say train 'em up and put 'em
on the Subs' bench – the soft sods
are, I'm told, reliably grammatical,
and some can spell, and punning
headlines might be up their street.

PHILISTINE

For every thousand people there's nine hundred doing the work, ninety doing well, nine doing good, and one lucky bastard who's the artist . . .

(Henry Carr in Tom Stoppard's *Travesties*)

I know it's a soft drainpipe,

but it could equally well be flabby
cock and balls, or elephant's trunk and ears –
a tease (pulley-adjustable) of curtain material.

My kind of cloth – I know
what to do with it, how to measure it,
cut it, line it, allow it to drop before stitching
the hem. I could twist it, ruche it,
let someone write about it.

I also know about the orange
that's not an orange because
it's a painting of an orange,
a brilliant orange and huge, you want
to squeeze out the juice and drink it.

A room under repair exhibits an
arrangement of paint-pots, plastic
sheeting and a pair of leaning tyres.
'Untitled' and a gloss would point out
what I need to bring to it.

As for the hanging whatever-it-is,
were I to withdraw its explanation,
unclasp its tie-back, and fit
a window in the wall behind it,
we should see St. Paul's.

THE END OF BRITISH FARMING

1

Rain is running down
Nelson's Column and Trafalgar Square
is awash with visitors inspecting the lions.

An American woman steps
into the National Gallery worried
about her camera lens. "This British weather

will be the end of us," she says,
as her husband shakes out the umbrellas.
In the Sackler room – Room 34 –

children with identical haircuts
sit on the wooden floor staring
at the British weather of long ago,

spread in oils with palette knives,
and they, too, ask why
it was always so fuzzy and cloudy.

One group sits around Turner's
Rain, Steam and Speed,
encouraged to express something

about the atmosphere of the piece.
"Does it make you shiver?" the instructor asks.
"It's like outside," a child replies.

But most are interested
in the hare running ahead of the train.
"Will it die?" "Where is it running *to*?"

The future? Constable's cornfield
was already a ghost, the country
delegates sing about at party conferences.

2

"There are ghosts here," says Will,
"and more Cockbains in the local
cemetery than anywhere else."

He's the same size as the chair
he's sitting in, waggling his stocking-soled feet,
and blowing out his lips.

"I think Margaret Thatcher
saw the guaranteed prices
farmers were getting and hated it.

And now, though it kills me,
we may have something to face:
there are too many sheep in the economy."

3

Brian's farm is a confusion
of mist and rotting leaves. He slams
the door of his Land Rover shut

and tastes the air. "The supermarkets
take the piss. Diversify?
Into what? Tenant farmers are no match

for the agribusiness people
who buy everything and turn it arable.
Up here the land is heavy clay."

4

A very English drizzle's
making a blur of Otford, hedges
loaded like wet sponges,

short grass squeaking underfoot.
There is mud in the road and mud
at the farm gate with a cold

whiteness in the Kent sky
that darkens quickly
in the afternoon. "Not so long ago,"

says Anne, "you could have 600 acres
and second-hand equipment
and send your kids to a good school."

Inside the family chapel, a book
records the lay ownership
of this piece of land from 1066

to 1521, the removal of the house
from a nobleman
to one of the wives of Henry VIII.

Across the way's
a disused cowshed Anne's father built
in 1946. Water drips from the lintel

and an inscription is carved above.
To the glory of agriculture, it says,
and the working man.

5

"People are gaining more
confidence in sushi," says the manager,
Trading Division, of Sainsbury's flagship

store in the Brompton Road.
In the meat department there is talk
of friendly farming practices. "Look!"

says Alison, a technical adviser, pointing to
a line of tank-green bottles of olive oil
stretching into the distance. "Choice!"

GROUCH

for Brian Jones

You once said that where we end up
is a pretty good indication of where
we were always going. By then
we've wasted time not recognising
who we are, or hoping it might be
otherwise, our pillowed heads
resisting what's insidiously true.

Someone I wouldn't give a letter to post
(and I was right) I later learned
I'd met with a grunt. My father
grunted, and I've been fighting him off
since then – something I choose
to do, because I tell myself I can.

Otherwise, who cares. If we stick around
long enough, we'll only turn into
the selves who stuck around, and few
would welcome being young again
without knowing what they know,
or knowing it, if that means knowing
where they're going is where they are.

THE GARDEN

Midnight under a fish-skin sky,
the cut-out dip and rise of blackened trees dropped in
for distance. Warnings come

with thick black borders like mass cards
for the dead. An untipped cigarette.
Silly to suppose there's life beyond those jokes of yours.

This kind of peace. Monk's straight-fingered
evergreen *'Round Midnight* will play for drinks tomorrow,
"The original is always best."

Here, the night-light spent, mild air is improvising
a disturbing calm. Find the poem you've been looking for,
plundered second-hand.

Death, it decides, becomes
a problem of style. How are we living still and vexed
by what we've achieved?

Two late bottles of London Pride help
create a reputation I can smile about. I take one chilled,
the other warm, then come inside.

Behind the central evergreen that you want rid of,
a brick shelter is your wine vault
and a cold retreat, its fat cigars for gardening

and driving home from taxing days.
Why should you want it seen?

A TOUCH OF LARYNGITIS

He ruined the practice. When
someone you've made a partner
puts cheques in front of you, you
sign them, don't you? The stubs
read differently . . . embezzlement.
However it was, he kept it up for years.
　I don't think, if he'd put his hands up,
I'd have chased him through the courts.
It isn't over yet. They've found
deposits running into hundreds
of thousands. He only took us
for 40K.
　　　I'd be retired by now,
writing stories. Remember the one
I read you when your pulse was racing?
You were very patient.
　　　I'll tell you where I'm going.
You'll never guess. Antarctica.
Pick up a ship at Buenos Aires,
and on the way back stop off at
South Georgia and the Falklands.
(Shackleton's a boyhood hero,
not at all like Scott. None of that
Edwardian class-bound stuff.)
It's an arm and a leg, I know,
for something temporary, but
that bastard's spoiled the rest,
even my leaving, left his smell
around the place.
　　　　　　Amoxicillin's
what you need. We're always talking.
I'm looking forward to the silence
and the cold . . .

THE SWEETMEAT

No one worried where the money came from,
nights like this were rare, to eat
so lavishly. Those in the upper village
listened to the drunken cheering, found it
sinister. The servants were behaving
oddly lately, less like servants.

He hoped his body would dissolve
like salt in water should he once take sides,
and that his children would dissolve.
You're as good as headman, he was told,
but no one noticed the old priest slip away
or that the sweetmeat he'd accepted lay untouched.

EL TIO DEL APARATO

Monsieur Trenchant the astrologer
saw what was coming through a hole

in his roof and had his pipe
knocked out of his mouth in the song

local kids sang as he passed.
He was gassed in the war and forgot

to go home with the tangle of red hair
he wore like wire. He was available

for lessons in his native French
but none of the girls would come.

The only foreigner anyone remembers
living here between the wars,

he was the man with the apparatus
who saw no one knows what

beyond the stars – until he disappeared
over the border perhaps into

Gibraltar and the stuff of dreams.

CHANNEL HOPPING

1

Here is a time for wanting
to write without irony,
to eliminate the wry
distance of humour, to let
the serious have its say,
free from the cushioned landing
that turns grimace into smile.

It's not as if the witty's
trivial, it's rather that
sometimes it seems a cheap way
out of facing up to life,
to squalor, sleaze and slaughter,
celebrity and clamour,
and the Sunday magazines.

2

Keeping catch isn't easy
for grizzly Alaskan bears
in summer. A single bear
can eat three-plus kilos worth
of salmon up in numbers
for a once-in-a-lifetime
chance to reproduce themselves,

but there are far too many
other bears, none of whom must
relish the congestion, or
stealing from another mouth –
yet this is the way things are,
join in or starve. We're wary
of bears lest they do us harm.

3

"What's the news from the White House,
Mark?" "Well, Anna, I'm afraid . . ."
Jesus! Is this some kind of
transcontinental garden
gate, a private audience?
Are we supposed to be here
listening? Should we go away

and let these people get on
with their sparkling other lives?
Their entitlement to fame?
Flamingos queue politely
for water safer than the
toxic, equatorial
stuff they find their algae in.

4

Olga who thinks she's human
is looking now for more than
a lap to lie in. Something's
wrong. It isn't rational
to suppose she's playing on
our sympathy. She's in pain.
It is no laughing matter,

nothing artful remedies
might cure, even if laughter
means we're a cut above bears.
She knows nothing about queues,
would freeze in Alaska, flee
from bigger bears. Perhaps there's
something in us she can see.

KINGFISHERS AND HERONS

When he climbed over the allotments' fence,
we asked him what he was doing. Going
fishing, he said. As long as it's only fish
you catch, and not the vegetables. I'm after
chub, he told us, and we let him through.

I saw luminous-blue and brown
kingfishers flying under the bridge.
He spoke of herons, too, a lock, and little waterfalls,
of all the patience fishing needs.

He was picking up the language bit by bit,
the right way round, doing and seeing,
before he learnt the names.

STEALING A SMOKE

I check the boilers regularly now –
a red light I report to John,
whose legs will be the death of him –

and I'm learning all the time, hot water
systems housing practical words
I had no interest in, like *sump*.

Down here is a maze of metal boxes,
pipes lagged with mottled silver, dials
and meters all with numbered tags

you can put names to on a draughtsman's plan
using the legend. Arrows point
this way and that, marked F and R.

Classrooms – beyond the *Schematic Layout's*
brief – are nonetheless heated by
the machinery it describes,

some so as you wouldn't notice, others
inducing sweat with all windows
open, and jackets on the backs

of chairs, such capricious distribution
as *de rigueur* as the reek of
cabbage in old style school canteens.

I peer through the porthole of Boiler One
gas has fired up of a sudden,
and imagine myself checking

flames as the stoker on a train I dreamed
when dreams of trains were all
I knew of heroes.

WORDS

1

Whether it was *farther* she wanted me to spell,
or *father*, I spelled out the wrong one every time,
preferring tears and the heroics of resistance
to the corner she'd put me in. There were other
classrooms off the corridor, but they
hadn't dawned on me yet.

2

I was made to sit next to Jane Oelman for the day.
My punishment for talking! Too beautiful for words,
she rolled her eyes when the only thing
I could think to ask her was the time.

3

As for the Deirdre Williams affair, I ended up
in front of Mr Burns, and Mum, and Mrs Williams,
not knowing then that Deirdre came from the Irish
meaning doubtful. I stood accused of something
rude and sexual, the Lord knows what.

SOMETHING TO SAY

What happens is strange. You look at the rules,
The octave and sestet, then the quatrain,
And the elaborate rhyme schemes, again
Stressing metrical feet, different schools
Of thought surrounding the tension between
The iamb and natural speech rhythms,
The tyranny of too many tee-tums,
And all the time remembering to mean.

Yet the form, far from being a constraint,
Its must-have-this-and-that standing in the way
Of sense, instead sets free by limiting,
Or seeming to limit, what one may say.
It's as durable as the Blues, singing
Through centuries. There's nothing that you mayn't!

SOMETHING NOW

Her mouth agape under a mask
that lines her face with sores,
her five stones floating on an ocean bed,
she's years past recognising those
she knew, will let go only at the third
behest of extreme unction, frail
fighter clinging on to life because
she knows it is in life we are required
to make our way, while an admiring nurse
apologises for another bruising round
of routine checks.
                         A new tyre
was being fitted to my Honda Civic
when the last Concorde flew over low,
its landing imminent. Someone called
and all those crowding the TV were suddenly
outside to peer up at the sky. A young
mechanic came back pleased he'd
something now to tell his grandchildren.

Mary could talk hers through a century
of speed and cyberspace, if she'd been
the least impressed by what was, after all,
a progress of convenience and nothing
to do with God.

AFTERWARDS

for Jude

You'll catch yourself for months making a mental note
of what to tell before recalling that, of course, you can't.
You'll do it anyway, for no one overhears the mind,

the tricks it plays. It will not be important, something
shameless, maybe, that might camouflage the disappointment
we suspect we are to those we love. I told my dad

about a goal at Brentford nine months on, and time enough
for someone to be born. For this is what it is to grieve,
to go on talking about nothing that could matter much.

AFRICAN NEGATIVES

for Alan Ross

The Best of Mobley's in the entrance hall,
with Paul Gonsalves, Oscar's *Night Train*,
Ernie Wilkins, hardback histories and more
– America second-hand and trestled,
the poems of Maya Angelou something new.

Out in the bar there's live jazz keen ears
can hear under the soundtrack's lush swell
for another Oscar, Wilde, half-hidden
by a colonnade, Bosie arriving
in a swoop of luggage: Paris on the turn.

The spine of Ross's book leaps out,
is mine for a back-pocket fiver, was
ten and six when it came out, old dosh.
I wave aside the 5p change to flick
the peach pages of a lover's find.

The black manager is searching through
a weight of keys, unlocks the cinema,
smiles only when she sees the wallet
lodged between our back-row seats –
library cards for Cambridge, London,

Manchester, Leeds. Plastic sesames
to Rare Reading Rooms! Then home,
a beer and Kenny Garrett's alto
on an eighteen quid CD. I know my jazz,
have most of what they had for sale.

Julian Joseph overflowed his stool,
found a sudden Latin groove in octaves
with the resident guitarist lost. He
was older, wider than I'd thought, perched
like that wiry Blue Note cover sketch

of Horace Silver on *Blowin' the Blues
Away* – not, as I could have sworn,
Song for My Father, probably because
my dad forgot things, too, without having to
to love, like Ross's couple in Bloemfontein:

*He not quite white
As she, nor she
So black as he*. It wasn't
a terminal complaint,
more like a matter of degree.

BIRDS

For me, it's never been the violence of size,
of eagles, or vultures, or crows, that petrifies

but the smaller species whirring invisible
electrical saws, mad flutterings, unable

to escape. A robin in a room's bad enough
if it's in a flap, but aviaries are the stuff

of nightmare. Dozens of the frantic things.
The thought of being in there, frozen trembling,

the glass they might fly headlong into!
I'd feel invisible and spare. I know I'm meant to

be beyond all this – I should be able to list
them, know their names, and could, if you insist,

consult the latest Field Guide, but I'd be lying
telling more than is the case – which is: it's flying,

the movement of wings, that makes me turn away
in terror (*They won't come, will they?*), and pray

they'll be kept in check. Hedren just freaked
when rehearsed in a cage of black-beaked

villains. I'm not surprised ornithophobia
set in. Mine's less clear: a rootless fear,

my mother thought, though Mr. Freud'd
say that simply telling the unembroidered

truth was going to be cure enough, or else
in the end it's sex like everything else.

THE NOOK

was on our landing
in the council house we shared
with the Battys, Mrs and a Mr
who's completely gone. They lived
downstairs. Even the garden
was cut in half by a path
that ran into a high brick wall. If
our ball would ever find itself
among her flowers, we'd have to
wait for its return, whenever,
though it was readily retrievable
the wrong side of a wire-mesh fence
that wasn't there. I once went down
to ask and couldn't remember
anything but getting out alive.
Compared to her the nook was nothing
but a black cave my brother'd
hide in to scare the life out of
our mother with a flashing grin.
It housed everything that was
occasional or spare, stuff I didn't
know about, and stuff I did, like
saws and mantles, coal and
the lemonade I took a swig from
that made me sick as you'd expect
for drinking turpentine. Now
it would be called something
old-fashioned like a larder,
and there'd be a light.

THE PENCIL FENCE

As symbols go, this one's fit
for purpose, as politicians say,
interminably, just as everything
they're involved in is robust,

and anyone who's anyone
is looking for the way forward,
as if we could step backwards
into the future they suppose

all those who disagree with them
are doing. Meanwhile the kids
inside the crumbling huts
behind the pencil fence go on

learning more than's fed them.
The pencil points look blunt,
though I daresay if you fell
on them from any height

the chances are you'd be
impaled, so they're waiting
for the health and safety reps
to reach the entry on their charts

that will see them off the premises.
But it's a novelty this fence,
it makes me smile, which matters
not at all. When the key stage cops

return, they'll have to have the fence's
point explained, though it will remain
lost on them because they'll not be able
to itemise what's learned in looking

on it, and they'll likely ask if
all the secondary schools are in
the throes of redesigning their fences
to resemble rows of ballpoint pens,

the fountain variety being dangerous,
of course. It's a wonder how a kid
makes it to school without an action plan.
It takes an arcane kind of skill.

THE MAN THEY NAMED AFTER HIS BED

for Norman (K1)

He wants to be discharged with nowhere to go.
They'll have to 'phone Social Services, find him
a bedsit, a place with wheelchair access.
They're doing nothing for him here. There's nothing
to be done but wait. He's off for a smoke.
And there's no let up to it. Sunderland lost
on penalties to Palace, twenty million
into the ether with a whistle's breath.
Who cares. He hates Newcastle, Alan Shearer.
It's bollocks, man. His orange running vest
is all he's left to wear. He's about to zoom
a bin bag full of stuff down to the local
laundrette. *Don't go away* he grins. Is gone.

AT BÉNÉVENT L'ABBAYE

I know enough to know
I don't know much. The translation
has *capitals* for *capitols*, and

assumes familiarity with naves
and transepts and a misspelt
narfhex. Under its cupola

I consult precise plans
in an attempt to work out
which are the *Absides Chapels*

and which one is the *South
Croissaisle*. The brief guide
continues: *Let us nom proceed*

to the *North Crossaisle*. The gold
number's everywhere, Divine
proportion, 1.618 –

in the nave, the chapels, even
the walls themselves, a great
but complex harmony

that rules druidical squares,
gold rectangles, *pentagones*,
and celtic cross. It is

decidedly a masterpiece
consecrated to "phi", another
mystery to look up

hopelessly. *You may
keep this for yourself
or put it back. Please*

do not throw it away.
I tell myself I shouldn't
dare. Best lose it in a file.

ORADOUR-SUR-GLANE

Dr Désourteaux's car's
a rustheap on the way
down to the village green.

Viewed from above
this Pollock canvas
is a box of human bones.

Ruins photograph
as burning paper, bodies
like blackened flakes.

Tramlines stick
to what they know,
expecting trams,

dolly camcorders
along a film-set
street. There are visitors

who cannot step
inside the church
for fear or superstition.

Seen, this cannot be
forgotten but what
produced it may be.

It's history and all
of history for some.
One disobedient

boy remembers
watching flames
flicker in the dark,

then tears, an amnesty,
and Leutnant Barth
admitting everything

and having no regrets.
The museum brightly lit
speaks several languages.

THE ANNUNCIATION

a figure in wood by Joseph Pyrz

He loves to touch her face, to feel
the tension in her neck, to trace
the gentle bellows of her miracle,
her faith, to hear a young boy
say her eyes are closed
because she's thinking hard.

He wonders if he should be
telling me a major supermarket
bought it for him when the Dean
enthused about her being
every woman, every race,
about the suffering engrained in
markings on her flawless face –
about a stained-glass window
paid for by a rival store.

What the boy responded to
was rapt attention, beauty,
polished wood, something
conspicuously new that breathed
life into Latin, Bede, and stone?
Not religion but a countenance
in which he saw his life was his?

My guide would say it was
the apprehension of divinity.
I've been away so long
I don't know what to think
that isn't bitter, except to say
this face, this shape, might
just as easily take breath away.

ROSENSTERN

It's difficult making your way
when you're confused at every turn.
Rosencrantz, they say, or is it
Guildenstern? We could die
for each other. This boat puts off
decisions, but we'll hand him over,
have to, in the end. What then?
We do as we're told. Our friend?
He was beyond us even then.

METAL MAN

Keep away, keep away, keep away from me
For I am the rocks of misery

I know it's anything but the hungry
want to hear fretting past me to a land
of plenty's welcoming light as if somehow
she were the old flame I'd never seen.
I point through Dead Man's panic-stricken gap
where water runs more swiftly than a dream.
My perch is stained but I'm beyond the sea,
will go on lasting and will never lie.
They will drown or not or lose their way
on land, no matter if I tell them how it is.
I eat the sky, can take or leave the rain.

TRUST

Transparency means everyone seeing
exactly what you're doing, accountability
living in a glasshouse hoping no one's
throwing stones. Knowing isn't enough
until, of course, you need someone
who knows, not just why or what, but how.
Watch carefully. Watch every move.

It's a shift in power. What is observable
expands while expertise shrinks in the light
of clipboards. Doctors live in fear of those
who teach their kids, teachers of parents
who can make them well. Compensation
stalks the high street, offering its services
for free. Don't you dare foul up. I'll sue!

Fifty-one weeks of the year, he's there,
selling straps and batteries. I leave him
easily the most expensive watch
I've ever owned, go to the bank, return,
and pay two quid. The time is right,
as is the date I stupidly dispute. He knows
I'm wrong but smiles and says I made him think.

FLUGEL

for Dick Pearce

What happened to the flugelhorn
you always played, that had you
turn down trumpet gigs, the famous
brother too brash, too much
like the army that could not
sustain itself on minor modal scales?

Did you buy yourself out, grow
your hair, practise, practise, find
the melting, mellow sound of
private life less trumpet loud, play
the fatter horn, because it caught
a quieter, self-effacing mood?

You were never one for soaring
high, preferring Miles to Dizzy
any day, Rollins to Bird. Is it
because bewildered in a world
you can't believe you helped create,
you must speak louder now?

So many lack technique, can only
marvel at a winged horn that puffs
the air with proof that gentle rain
can slake a giant thirst. Did it grow
too comfortable, so much the salve
you locked away its charm for good?

As if suddenly you were a sophist
duping those who'll follow any lure
that takes them out beyond the boom
of modern gods towards the human
birdsong that's heartsease if only
temporarily, then temporarily at least.

SIX FOR CRICKET

1. Invitation, 1845

Turnham Green Albion Club
will be happy to make a match
with any village eleven –
not too strong.

2. The Old Pack Horse, 1853

Forget for a moment,
if you will, the thin red line,
Bleak House, a cholera
epidemic and Victoria's

epidural, and concentrate
instead on Blackman's
pub and the gentlemen
gathered there (including

the local undertaker and
a man called Caught)
and you'll be witnessing
another birth ...

3. May and August, 1856

Weather magnificently fine.
Having had recourse to every
species of paltry manoeuvring
to waste time and make it

a drawn game, Staines Albion
started for home at half-past eleven.
Tuftnell Park players arrived late,
and in a staggering manner

one and two at a time from all
points of the compass, finished
seven down for 76 and went back
whence they'd come around eleven.

4. For Charity, 1926

The Mayor of Hammersmith
has just been clean bowled
in his top hat, coat and insignia,
sans gloves or pads or box.

Still in his crease, he's waving
to the crowd behind a whiskered
grin, while a gloved and padded,
similarly-hatted keeper

looks down on the ball
as on the rummest creature.
A smiling umpire's on his way
to find the bails.

5. Liberation

After Greer and Thatcher,
the Hayburn Cup went to a lady,
namely, Audrey Deery, for her
unstinting efforts making teas.

6. An Opponent at Fuller's, May 22nd 2004

Now someone's in the wars
with a twisted ankle, more
of a soccer complaint. He
will not be consoled.

The rest of his team is in
the field and he may not
be able to bat. There's no one
here to share his grief.

Not even a twelfth man.

ON MAGRITTE'S 'Man of the Sea' (1926)

> *For the student of literature who asked which*
> *bits of* David Copperfield *he should read.*

I'm a diver in black with bulges in all the right places
except where it matters. My head is musical, a pre-shaped

violin. I am obsessed with bits of wood, cross sections
of latticed table, painters' palettes, and the jigsaw cut-outs

I stand on to lever open a plane door to a paler sky
that has ignored its meeting with the sea. A stone corner-piece

suggests the fireplace complete. It's all we need. The gist.
Why waste time on the whole affair? We know the stories

of table, fireplace, floor, hear the music of sea and sky
from a bar or two. I read only dust-jackets, consult synopses

in my guide to films. You'll say no one can tell the final score
five minutes into the match, and I'll concede that's sometimes true,

but not nearly often enough to warrant ninety minutes,
extra time, or five days in extremis for a draw. Get it

over with. Move on. Nothing's worth the time it takes.
I don't need ears or nose or mouth. I know a block

of solid sand shifts somewhere beneath my feet, that it will
crack like ice and in my element there'll be no more of me.

GOING

There is apparently significance
in numbers. Thirty years
is a carriage clock. There are those

who ensure they're never seen
again where they've been paid to be,
who start up other lives,

but the end of things is nothing
else to go to beyond whatever
is believed, and is the case

for all of us, members of one club
or another whether we choose
to join or not. Or leave.

The good in us will always
forget. It's nothing
rotten in our state. It's

the way we are, and clocks
ignore us everywhere we look,
or cry, or celebrate, or think

somehow we could have
made things right. Some people
have the carriage clock

some time before they leave,
before they know that going
is arriving somewhere else.

THERE'S ALWAYS THIS

She is wearing money and straight black hair,
and, standing close, looks up at him, is kissed,
a million miles away from mortgages
and kids, though not, perhaps, from paying cash
and nannies. On a Metro station, they
believe in love, for it's themselves they love
for capturing each other. Suddenly,
there are people on platforms everywhere
I look, kissing, and on Eurostar where
a high-heeled blonde won't leave her stubbled beau
alone for long, will thread a bangled arm
around his neck and bare her perfect teeth.
Speed turns up the volume on the outside
world, and snow is angling to come in.

THE GOOD CATHOLIC

Miss Robinson ruled her Tea Rooms like a headmistress
in a black dress down to her ankles, her pet monkey –
chained to the door of the oven range – grabbing coins
from customers and storing them in its bulging jaws.

I'd half-a-crown, a fortune that I showed and lost.
I slapped the creature good and soundly, hoping
I'd be linked by no one to its piercing scream,
and boasted it remembered me. I wanted to be free.

Next door in the picture theatre, the monkey
will not let me be. It revels in its right to misbehave.
By the time Messala bites the dust, I've had enough
of Judah Ben-Hur and being good. I want it dead.

ANTIQUITY HALL

Have in mind the horses' necessary patience, when
the pub door opened directly on to the hithe;

or Tom Hearne and friends smoking honest pipes,
sharing a poor opinion of Captain Steele and Whigs;

and wonder what they or the bargees would make
of the local businessmen who like to drop in

for a quiet drink while Elizabeth is left to ship
a secular dissent Great Anna wouldn't recognize;

or of the flashing fruit machine that shows a line
of Kings to someone lucky, on a break from hustling

at the table you must lift your head from
to see the giant screen. Honest folk were never here.

I cycle past this place I'm rooted in each day
and not the once an artist might suggest he's caught.

It's somewhere people live their lives and die,
become the heritage and history you like to dwell upon.

A MARKET TOWN

Anywhere can get significant,
a promontory settlement
where church and corn mill
look out over market square,
somewhere on the way
to somewhere else, that
out of nothing spirits tradesmen,
shops and stalls, and iron forges,
survives a lethal ford, the plague
and civil strife, and engages
in successive acts of self-
improvement with the help
of local benefactors and its
being a perfect spot for artists,
poets and the like and those
who seek the picturesque.
Streets get cleaned and widened,
health is insisted on by law,
as is responsibility, and a style,
mock-Gothic, say, adopted
with an early eye for visitors.
The railway was a crushing
blow and with it the decline
in navigation but The King's Head
and The Coffee House keep up
their squeaky signs. People
rarely know what they are
looking at. They carry bags,
wear shorts in summer,
window-shop. Cars snake
through narrow streets and
passageways, park up close

against a wall, somewhere
they'll fit, and accidental locals
walk through photo albums
far and near, know this
is how things need to be.
Most of us are pleased
I think the place exists.

LADY TANSFIELD'S MEMORIAL

It looks idyllic, church and cottages
and across the green the almshouses,
but you don't know the half of it.
She commandeered a whole chapel
for that memorial, that monstrous,
garish thing for her husband as if
he was worth remembering, unless
as one who lined his pockets
at his inferiors' expense.

No wonder it took two whole centuries
before the residents stopped burning him
each year. But awful though it is,
just look at what went into making it,
the craftsmanship of those responsible,
that skill in carving. Was the emaciated
skeleton you can see if you stoop down
and look underneath their little joke,
reminding us we all end up the same?

Then there were the incarcerated
mutineers, three hundred and forty of them
up from Salisbury till they were caught
and locked inside. What sort of a use
for a church is that? And all for what,

for suggesting the people might agree?
Those pamphlets taught the English
how to write in their own language,
but people get put down. They always do.

And what did Morris get so fussed about?
Not people, anyway, but mediaeval
wall paintings! That vicar had his head
on straight, the one he said he'd stand on
if he had a mind to because it was *his*
church. Things won't ever change.
Names get remembered, not those
who crafted for them. There's no
reason in it. None.

SILENCE AND TWILIGHT

A rosary of cars slips down the street
towards St Lawrence's aerial pile
in summer under a still sky whose heat
converts a rainbow range into a white-roofed file
in search of somewhere suitable to park,
those settled in already bowling dark

jagged shadows under rolling chassis.
Death is anxiety in this breathless
light, suffocation for the lack of breeze,
fever not hypothermia, a loneliness
that persists in the company of friends,
wanting something before the whole thing ends.

Wool built this church with its pomegranate
badge of Aragon, its memorial –
brasses, carvings, perpendicular plan, its
later evidence of fire, that grotesque gargoyle
exterior, the empty niche that held
the Virgin Mary Cromwellians felled,

its added sixteenth century spire. Until
Catherine had the church renamed it was
St Mary's. Back then religion was still
necessary, and should be even now because
innately we're religious after all –
or so says the latest controversial

philosopher who believes denying
God's like repressing sex, which isn't much
to those who can't believe, those trying
not to say it's all a con, and needing to clutch
on to something more than supermarket
shopping, and remembering where they're parked.

SHOOTING KOFI ANNAN IN DARFUR

What's to tell the pictures do not tell? You've
seen the photograph, its uncanny matchstick figures
starved saplings and its forest a slow march
of migrants merging like freckles on sun-drenched skin.

All I wanted was a fag. I dropped one in the mud.
People can tut in restaurants, but I can see myself
inhale in slowmo, exhale relief, like coming up for air.
Our camp was half an hour away. We were glad of the walk.

Later, I turned to see a boy holding up for me to take
the cigarette he had retrieved from mud. He placed it
in my palm and disappeared before I could demean
his generosity with money, speech, or tears.

THIS IS ME

Briskly on to the train, long legs in jeans
and toe-scuffed boots inspected lovingly.
Make-up bag. All sorts. To have to do this
every day. Cream under the eyes and powder,
giant brush. I'm watching, trying not to,
in the window opposite. She has her compact.
I imagine she conducts her whole life briskly,
would stare right through me if I turned to see.

*

Eating up the platform she is bawling filth
for everyone to hear though it's her bloke
she's bawling at. Who cares? She wants him
there when she arrives. He's talking shit.

*

Her dress is brake-light red, her lips, her shoes.
She's forty and between relationships. Who wants her
kids? Soon, eventually, by heart, she will perform
her poems and I'll wander off behind a wall.
The words improve with nothing in the way.

MARGARET BY THE FIRE

Mum had taken her in for her to sit on the rug
in front of the fire doing nothing. I listened to her

being talked about, how she wasn't moving
a muscle to find a job. I got into trouble once

for saying as much to her face. She was like
a whey-faced pet, had something to do

with Mickey, a good-for-nothing weasel
of a man Dad said was nothing more

than she deserved. She'll be dead by now
but resurrects herself. I'd read Mickey's

athletics' programmes while the adults talked
of stuff I hadn't a clue about, like de Valera.

He was not to be confused with Mick,
the man we reached through hushed corridors

in Hammersmith. I was made to sit
in an anteroom with nothing to do

but marvel at a height of ceiling
and the weight of wood in the doors.

When Dad came out, we hurried home,
his turn-ups flapping against his ankles.

This Mick was clearly not the sort of man
who'd want to be dealing with Margaret.

LISTEN HERE

While the opening credits of *Last Tango* rolled,
I whispered this was Gato Barbieri, later that the arranger
must be Oliver Nelson.

I did it again when I heard Billy Joel's
Just The Way You Are. That alto solo
has to be Phil Woods'.

The point is not that I'm insufferable,
but that they're recognizable a few bars in
from anywhere.

LETTER TO JOHN HOYLAND

i.m. Robert Motherwell (1915 - 1991)

You called Bob's *Elegy* motif the Bulls' Bollocks,
its black leaking verticals and tuberous ovoids floating
on white and the colours of the Spanish flag, so many
versions of the same idea, over a hundred, and none
political, but rather his *insistence that a terrible
death happened that should not be forgot.*

When his prize cases of Mouton Rothschild '74 arrived
he heard the ultimatum that he must give up the drink
or die. What was there left to do but write and talk and
paint until, no longer the black sheep, he could confront
his problem canvasses with pots of money in the bank,
and value your opinion no holds barred, till blotted out?

EVEN BEFORE A CERTAIN AGE

The idea started with the grandchildren –
knitting for adults takes too long,
and it's seldom wanted – and it's odd
the things one turns a hand to helping out.
We used to sit and talk. Well, I'd talk
and he'd listen, he tells me now.

Now I knit with the TV on while he gets on
with his work, or reads. He's the only
straight amongst the thirty-strong committee
of a charity for ageing dancers. This is
my last year for a while at least,
arranging sponsorship, that sort of thing.

Ashkenazy's here conducting Shostakovich
so I've got to get the polyfilla out
for drinks before. We'll meet up later –
me and my husband, not Ashkenazy,
though that's possible at drinks – to hear
some soporific Norwegian piano 'jazz'.

Is it jazz, I wonder? I've heard it all before.
This kind of chit-chat passes the time.
It's failsafe till you ask what was my name
before I married and the floodgates open.
We all have complicated lives.

Levity is easier, like working out if my idea
for a company called Norfolk Knits
might not best describe arranging sponsorship
and the bonhomie of drinks before.
Already there's a Norfolk Frock Exchange.

WHAT SHE SAID

Heaven only knows what they were talking about at Harvard
before the smoke had cleared but one blonde and leggy student
striding purposefully out of class and clutching books lovingly
like a shoulder bag, stopped so abruptly to upbraid her blonde
and leggy student-friend I had to pull up short. B*ut, Julia, that's so
September Tenth.* I can't think why I should suppose that Heaven knows,
but if it doesn't, isn't, then living is more serious than we thought.
Stilled, I watched them striding on and giggling, linking arms.

FIRST FLIGHT

for Colin & Diana Miller

Every generation discovers ice, Icarus falling
from a marble sky he thought himself attached to,
that fire burns no matter who your dad is,
and that breathing-in the triumph is a cut above
the fancy dress of taking everyone's advice.
Bronze is heavier than air, and more expensive.
Survival's shortfall comes with learning
someone got there first, that every muscle's
been stretched as far as it'll bear before, that better
toning's led to faster times and longer lives.
Flying's humdrum nowadays, a kind of ice,
as if falling's failure were a form of hope,
and falling now took longer than it did.

Notes & Further Acknowledgements

'The End of British Farming', save for some minor amendments and reorderings, is excerpted from Andrew O'Hagan's essay, 'The End of British Farming', (London Review of Books, Vol.23 No.6: 22 March 2001, pp.3-16). I have O'Hagan's blessing for this.

El Tio del Aparato: The Man with the Apparatus

African Negatives by Alan Ross (Eyre & Spottiswoode, 1962)

'Six for Cricket': My thanks to Dewi Humphries for *The History of Turnham Green Cricket Club 1853-2003* and the TGCC Fixture List and Handbook 2004, from both of which the poem draws. Warwick Draper's *Chiswick* (Philip Allan, 1932) and Gillian Clegg's *Chiswick Past* (Historical Publications, 1995) were also sources.

'Antiquity Hall', 'A Market Town', 'Lady Tansfield's Memorial' and 'Silence & Twilight' began life as responses to watercolours by Frank Palmer. 'Silence & Twilight' alludes to and borrows the form of Shelley's 'A Summer Evening Churchyard', which also refers to Lechlade in Gloucestershire.

'The Good Catholic' and 'Metal Man' make some use of material from John Cowell's *Sligo: Land of Yeats' Desire* (The O'Brien Press).

'The Annunciation': Pyrz's sculpture may be found in Durham Cathedral's Galilee Chapel

'Letter to John Hoyland': The elegy referred to is Robert Motherwell's repeated *Elegy to the Spanish Republic.* Since 1946, each year the Chateau Mouton Rothschild label has been designed by a famous living artist. Motherwell's year was 1974. Payment always takes the form of cases of the relevant year's wine.

'First Flight': Colin Miller's sculpture of the same name is a source.